# The Hidden Truths of Banking Contracts

Joseph Rodriguez

Published by Joseph Rodriguez, 2024.

THE HIDDEN TRUTHS OF BANKING CONTRACTS

**First edition. October 8, 2024.**



ISBN: 979-8227283696

Written by Joseph Rodriguez.

# Table of Contents

# The Hidden Truths
## of
## Banking Contracts:
## A Guide to Protecting
## Your Financial Rights
### By Joseph Rodriguez, PhD

# Chapter 1: The Foundations of a Valid Contract

In the complex world of banking and finance, understanding the basic principles of contract law is crucial. Whether you're opening a new account, taking out a loan, or disputing a charge, you're dealing with contracts. This chapter will explore the essential elements that make a contract legally binding, with a special focus on the concept of consideration. We'll also examine real-world cases where banking contracts have been deemed invalid, providing valuable lessons for consumers and financial professionals alike.

### Elements of a Legally Binding Contract

A contract, in its simplest form, is an agreement between two or more parties that creates mutual obligations enforceable by law. However, not all agreements are legally binding contracts. For a contract to be valid and enforceable, it must contain several key elements:

1. Offer: One party must make a clear proposal to enter into an agreement.

2. Acceptance: The other party must accept the terms of the offer unequivocally.

3. Consideration: Both parties must exchange something of value (more on this later).

4. Capacity: All parties must have the legal ability to enter into a contract.

5. Intention: There must be a mutual intention to create a legally binding agreement.

6. Legality: The purpose and terms of the contract must be legal.

In the banking context, these elements manifest in specific ways. For example, when a bank offers a loan, it's making an offer. When you sign the loan agreement, you're indicating your acceptance. The loan amount is the bank's consideration, while your promise to repay with interest is your consideration.

### The Concept of Consideration in Contract Law

Consideration is a fundamental principle in contract law and is particularly relevant in banking contracts. It refers to something of value that each party gives or promises to the other. This "something of value" can be money, goods, services, or even a promise to do (or not do) something.

### In banking, consideration often takes the form of:

- The bank providing a loan or line of credit
- The customer promising to repay the loan with interest
- The bank offering account services
- The customer agreeing to maintain a minimum balance or pay fees

It's important to note that consideration doesn't have to be of equal value between the parties. The law generally doesn't concern itself with whether each party made a good bargain, only that some form of consideration exists.

### Example: Consideration in a Mortgage Contract

In a mortgage contract, the consideration is clear:

- The bank's consideration: Providing the loan amount to purchase the property

- The borrower's consideration: Promising to repay the loan with interest and using the property as collateral

### Case Studies: When is a Banking Contract Invalid?

Understanding when a contract might be deemed invalid is crucial for protecting your rights. Let's examine some real-world cases where banking contracts were challenged:

Case 1: Lack of Capacity - Smith v. National Bank (2018)

In this case, an elderly customer with diagnosed dementia entered into a complex investment agreement with a bank. The court ruled the contract invalid due to the customer's lack of capacity to understand the terms.

Lesson: Banks have a responsibility to ensure their customers have the capacity to enter into agreements, especially for complex financial products.

Case 2: Misrepresentation - Johnson v. Credit Corp (2019)

A bank was found to have misrepresented the terms of a loan, stating a lower interest rate in verbal discussions than what was in the written contract. The court held that this misrepresentation invalidated the contract.

Lesson: Always read the written terms carefully and don't rely solely on verbal assurances.

Case 3: Lack of Consideration - Brown v. Savings & Loan (2020)

A bank attempted to enforce new account fees without providing any new or additional services. The court found there was no consideration for these new fees, rendering that part of the contract unenforceable.

Lesson: Banks must provide something of value in exchange for fees or changes to existing agreements.

Understanding the foundations of a valid contract is your first line of defense in managing your financial relationships. By knowing what makes a contract binding and what can invalidate it, you're better equipped to protect your rights and interests.

In the next chapter, we'll delve deeper into the specific nature of bank credits, building on this foundation to explore how banks create and manage the very lifeblood of our financial system.

# Chapter 2: Decoding Bank Credits

In the previous chapter, we explored the foundations of valid contracts. Now, we delve into the heart of banking operations: bank credits. Understanding bank credits is crucial for anyone navigating the financial world, as they form the basis of most banking transactions. This chapter will demystify the concept of bank credits, explain how they're created, and discuss their various forms and implications.

### What are Bank Credits?

At its core, a bank credit is a bookkeeping entry that represents a bank's promise to provide funds to an individual or entity. It's important to understand that bank credits are not physical currency, but rather accounting entries that represent value.

### Key Characteristics of Bank Credits:

1. Intangibility: Bank credits exist as electronic records, not physical assets.

2. Transferability: They can be moved between accounts and institutions.

3. Creation through lending: Most bank credits are created when banks make loans.

4. Basis for money supply: Bank credits form a significant part of the modern money supply.

The Process of Credit Creation in Modern Banking

The creation of bank credits is a process that often surprises people when they first learn about it. Contrary to popular belief, banks do not simply lend out money that has been deposited by other customers.

### Steps in Credit Creation:

1. Loan Application: A customer applies for a loan.

2. Approval: The bank approves the loan based on the customer's creditworthiness and other factors.

3. Credit Creation: The bank creates a new deposit in the borrower's account, effectively creating new money.

4. Double-Entry Bookkeeping: The bank records the loan as both an asset (the borrower's obligation to repay) and a liability (the new deposit).

This process is often referred to as "credit creation out of thin air" because the bank is not transferring pre-existing funds, but creating new credits.

Example:

If Bank A grants a $100,000 mortgage to Customer X, it doesn't transfer $100,000 from its reserves. Instead, it creates a new deposit of $100,000 in X's account. Bank A's balance sheet now shows:

- Assets: +$100,000 (loan to X)

- Liabilities: +$100,000 (deposit in X's account)

Different Types of Bank Credits and Their Implications

Bank credits come in various forms, each with its own characteristics and implications for both the bank and the customer.

1. Demand Deposits

- Description: Checking accounts, savings accounts

- Characteristics: Immediately available for withdrawal

- Implications: Forms part of the narrowest measure of money supply (M1)

2. Time Deposits

- Description: Certificates of Deposit (CDs), term deposits

- Characteristics: Locked in for a specific period, often with higher interest rates

- Implications: Less liquid, part of broader money supply measures (M2, M3)

3. Lines of Credit

- Description: Credit cards, overdraft protection

- Characteristics: Revolving credit, can be used and repaid repeatedly

- Implications: Creates potential for cyclical debt, affects credit scores

4. Loans

- Description: Mortgages, personal loans, business loans
- Characteristics: Fixed amount, specific repayment terms
- Implications: Creates new money in the economy, basis for credit creation

### The Impact of Bank Credits on the Economy

The creation and circulation of bank credits have far-reaching effects on the broader economy:

1. Money Supply: Bank credits significantly expand the money supply beyond physical currency.

2. Economic Growth: By providing credits, banks enable investments and spending that drive economic activity.

3. Inflation: Excessive credit creation can lead to inflation if not matched by economic output.

4. Financial Stability: The interconnected nature of bank credits can lead to systemic risks, as seen in the 2008 financial crisis.

### Legal and Regulatory Considerations

The creation and management of bank credits are subject to various regulations:

1. Reserve Requirements: Banks must hold a certain percentage of deposits as reserves.

2. Capital Requirements: Banks must maintain specific ratios of capital to risk-weighted assets.

3. Lending Limits: Restrictions on how much a bank can lend to a single borrower.

4. Transparency Rules: Requirements for disclosing terms and conditions of credit products.

Bank credits are the invisible force that powers much of our financial system. By understanding how they're created, their various forms, and their implications, you're better equipped to navigate your financial relationships with banks. This knowledge is crucial when examining the validity of banking contracts and transactions.

In the next chapter, we'll explore the origin and nature of bank credits in more detail, including the controversial topic of fractional reserve banking.

# Chapter 3: The Origin and Nature of Bank Credits

In the previous chapter, we explored what bank credits are and how they function in the modern banking system. Now, we'll delve deeper into the origin and nature of these credits. Understanding how banks generate credits and the system that allows this process is crucial for anyone seeking to comprehend the foundations of our financial system. This chapter will explore the mechanics of credit generation, the fractional reserve banking system, and the ethical and legal considerations surrounding these practices.

## How Banks Generate Credits

The process of credit generation by banks is a topic that often sparks debate and confusion. To understand this process, we need to examine the unique role banks play in our economy.

### The Money Multiplier Effect

Banks have the ability to create money through a process known as the money multiplier effect. Here's how it works:

1. Initial Deposit: A customer deposits money into a bank.

2. Reserve Requirement: The bank keeps a fraction of this deposit as a reserve (as required by law) and lends out the rest.

3. New Deposit: The borrowed money is spent and eventually deposited in another bank account.

4. Repeat: This process continues, with each new deposit allowing for more lending.

Through this process, the initial deposit can lead to a much larger increase in the money supply.

### Example of the Money Multiplier Effect

Let's say the reserve requirement is 10% and someone deposits $1,000:

1. Bank A keeps $100 as reserve and lends $900

2. The $900 is spent and deposited in Bank B

3. Bank B keeps $90 as reserve and lends $810

4. This continues...

In this scenario, the initial $1,000 deposit could potentially lead to $10,000 in new money creation.

**The Fractional Reserve Banking System**

The ability of banks to generate credits is fundamentally tied to the fractional reserve banking system. This system allows banks to hold only a fraction of their deposits in reserve and lend out the rest.

Key Features of Fractional Reserve Banking:

1. Reserve Ratio: Banks are required to keep a certain percentage of deposits as reserves.

2. Money Creation: Banks can lend out more money than they have in deposits.

3. Liquidity Risk: There's a risk if too many depositors want to withdraw funds simultaneously.

4. Central Bank Support: Central banks act as lenders of last resort to prevent bank runs.

Advantages of Fractional Reserve Banking:

- Enables economic growth by increasing the money supply

- Allows banks to earn profits through lending

- Provides liquidity to the economy

Disadvantages of Fractional Reserve Banking:

- Can lead to bank runs if confidence in a bank falters

- May contribute to economic instability and boom-bust cycles

- Raises ethical questions about money creation

**Ethical and Legal Considerations in Credit Origination**

The ability of banks to create money through credit origination raises several ethical and legal questions.

Ethical Considerations:

1. Wealth Distribution: Does the ability to create money give banks unfair economic power?

2. Risk to Depositors: Is it ethical for banks to use depositors' money for lending?

3. Economic Stability: Does this system contribute to economic instability?

Legal Considerations:

1. Regulatory Oversight: How should governments regulate banks' ability to create money?

2. Transparency: Should banks be required to disclose their money creation activities?

3. Consumer Protection: How can borrowers be protected from predatory lending practices?

### Alternative Views on Bank Credit Creation

It's important to note that there are differing views on how bank credit creation works. While the fractional reserve model is widely taught, some economists argue for alternative models.

The Credit Creation Theory of Banking

This theory suggests that banks create new money whenever they make loans, regardless of their reserves. According to this view:

- Banks don't wait for deposits to make loans

- Loans create deposits, rather than deposits enabling loans

- The central bank accommodates the demand for reserves after the fact

### Implications of the Credit Creation Theory:

- Banks have even more power to influence the money supply

- The role of reserve requirements is less significant

- Monetary policy may need to focus more on regulating lending practices

### Legal Status of Bank-Created Money

The legal status of bank-created money is complex and varies by jurisdiction. In most countries:

- Bank deposits are recognized as legal money

- Banks have a legal right to create credit, subject to regulations

- Central banks have the authority to regulate credit creation

However, the exact legal framework can be ambiguous, leading to debates and legal challenges.

The origin and nature of bank credits are foundational to understanding modern finance. The ability of banks to generate credits through the fractional reserve system has profound implications for our economy, raising important ethical and legal questions.

As we've seen, the process of credit creation is complex and sometimes controversial. Different theories exist about how exactly this process works, and the legal and ethical implications continue to be debated.

In the next chapter, we'll explore how these bank credits are valued and what they represent in terms of real-world assets. This will help us further understand the nature of banking transactions and the claims banks can make based on these credits.

# Chapter 4: Valuation and Representation of Bank Credits

In the previous chapters, we explored the nature of bank credits, how they are created, and the system that allows for their generation. Now, we turn our attention to a crucial question: What do these credits actually represent, and how are they valued? This chapter will delve into the complex world of bank credit valuation, examining how these intangible assets relate to real-world value, and the role of central banks in shaping this system.

### Understanding the True Value of Bank Credits

Bank credits, as we've discussed, are essentially promises made by banks—promises to pay a certain amount of money on demand or at a specified time. But what gives these promises value?

Factors Influencing the Value of Bank Credits:

1. Trust in the Banking System: The value of bank credits is fundamentally based on the public's trust in the banking system.

2. Government Backing: In many countries, bank deposits are insured by the government, adding an extra layer of security.

3. Assets Backing the Credits: Banks hold various assets (loans, securities, reserves) that theoretically back their credit obligations.

4. Economic Conditions: The overall state of the economy affects the value and stability of bank credits.

5. Regulatory Framework: Strong banking regulations can increase confidence in bank credits.

### The Concept of Fiat Money

To understand the value of bank credits, we need to grasp the concept of fiat money:

- Fiat money is currency that a government has declared to be legal tender.

- It is not backed by a physical commodity (like gold), but rather by the government that issued it.

- Bank credits, in many ways, function as a form of fiat money.

**How Bank Credits Relate to Tangible Assets**

While bank credits themselves are intangible, they do have relationships to tangible assets in several ways:

1. Loans and Mortgages

When a bank creates credits by issuing a loan or mortgage, these credits are often tied to tangible assets:

- A mortgage is secured by real estate.

- A car loan is secured by the vehicle.

- Business loans may be secured by company assets.

2. Bank Reserves

A portion of bank credits is backed by the bank's reserves, which may include:

- Physical currency in bank vaults

- Deposits with the central bank

- Highly liquid securities

3. Investment Portfolios

Banks often invest a portion of their assets in various financial instruments:

- Government bonds

- Corporate securities

- Other financial assets

These investments provide another layer of tangible backing to bank credits.

## The Role of Central Banks and Monetary Policy

Central banks play a crucial role in determining the value and stability of bank credits through their monetary policy actions.

Key Functions of Central Banks:

1. Setting Interest Rates: This affects the cost of borrowing and the value of money.

2. Open Market Operations: Buying or selling government securities to influence the money supply.

. Reserve Requirements: Mandating how much banks must hold in reserves.

4. Lender of Last Resort: Providing emergency liquidity to banks in crisis.

**How Monetary Policy Affects Bank Credit Value:**

- Expansionary Policy: When central banks lower interest rates or increase the money supply, it tends to decrease the value of existing bank credits relative to goods and services (inflation).

- Contractionary Policy: When central banks raise interest rates or decrease the money supply, it tends to increase the value of existing bank credits relative to goods and services (deflation).

## Quantifying Bank Credits: Accounting and Reporting

Banks use specific accounting methods to quantify and report on their credits:

1. Balance Sheet Reporting

- Assets: Loans, investments, and reserves

- Liabilities: Deposits and other obligations

- Equity: The bank's own capital

2. Fair Value Accounting

Banks are often required to report the "fair value" of their assets and liabilities, which can affect how credits are valued.

3. Loan Loss Provisions

Banks must estimate and account for potential losses on their loan portfolios, which impacts the overall value of their credit assets.

## Challenges in Valuing Bank Credits

Several factors make the valuation of bank credits challenging:

1. Intangibility: The inherent nature of bank credits as promises rather than physical assets.

2. Complexity: The intricate web of financial relationships in modern banking.

3. Time Discrepancy: The mismatch between short-term liabilities (deposits) and long-term assets (loans).

4. Market Fluctuations: Changes in interest rates and economic conditions can rapidly affect credit values.

5. Systemic Risk: The interconnected nature of the banking system means individual bank credits are affected by system-wide factors.

### Legal and Regulatory Considerations

The valuation and representation of bank credits are subject to various legal and regulatory requirements:

1. Accounting Standards: Banks must adhere to specific accounting rules (e.g., GAAP, IFRS) in reporting their credits.

2. Disclosure Requirements: Banks are often required to provide detailed information about their credit portfolios.

3. Capital Adequacy Rules: Regulations like Basel III require banks to maintain certain ratios of capital to risk-weighted assets.

4. Stress Testing: Regulators often require banks to undergo stress tests to assess the resilience of their credit portfolios.

The valuation and representation of bank credits is a complex topic that lies at the heart of modern finance. While bank credits may seem abstract, they are intimately connected to real-world assets and economic activities. Understanding how these credits are valued and what they represent is crucial for anyone seeking to navigate the financial system effectively.

As we've seen, the value of bank credits is not solely determined by the banks themselves, but is influenced by a wide range of factors, including government policies, economic conditions, and regulatory frameworks. This complexity underscores the importance of transparency and robust oversight in the banking system.

In the next chapter, we'll explore the practical implications of these concepts by examining how banks transfer and manage these credits in day-to-day operations.

# Chapter 5: Possession and Transfer of Bank Credits

In our previous chapters, we've explored the nature, creation, and valuation of bank credits. Now, we turn our attention to a critical aspect of banking operations: how banks actually possess and transfer these credits. This chapter will delve into the complexities of credit possession in the modern banking system, the mechanisms of credit transfer, and the legal and practical implications of these processes.

## When Do Banks Actually "Possess" Credits?

The concept of "possession" when it comes to bank credits is not as straightforward as it might seem. Unlike physical currency, bank credits exist primarily as electronic records.

Types of Credit Possession:

1. Legal Possession: Banks have legal claim to the credits they create or acquire.

2. Operational Possession: The ability to use, transfer, or leverage credits in banking operations.

3. Regulatory Possession: Meeting regulatory requirements for holding certain levels of credits or capital.

## The Paradox of Credit Possession

Interestingly, banks can be said to "possess" credits even before they are created. This is because:

- Banks have the authority to create credits through lending.

- Regulatory frameworks allow banks to operate with fractional reserves.

- The act of lending itself generates new credits.

This paradox is at the heart of many debates about the nature of money and banking.

## The Electronic Nature of Modern Banking

Modern banking is predominantly electronic, which has profound implications for how credits are possessed and transferred.

Key Aspects of Electronic Banking:

1. Digital Ledgers: Most bank credits exist only as entries in digital accounting systems.

2. Real-Time Processing: Many transactions are processed almost instantaneously.

3. Interconnected Systems: Banks are linked through various networks and clearing systems.

Implications for Credit Possession:

- The concept of physical possession becomes largely irrelevant.

- "Possession" is more about having the authority and ability to manipulate digital records.

- The speed of electronic transfers can blur the lines of when a bank actually "possesses" credits.

### Mechanisms of Credit Transfer

Banks transfer credits through various mechanisms, each with its own characteristics and implications.

1. Interbank Transfers

- Process: Banks transfer credits between themselves through clearing systems.

- Examples: SWIFT, Fedwire, CHAPS

- Implications: These transfers can affect banks' reserve positions and liquidity.

2. Customer Transactions

- Process: Credits are transferred between customer accounts, either within the same bank or between different banks.

- Examples: Wire transfers, ACH transfers, online banking transactions

- Implications: These transactions don't typically affect the overall amount of credits in the banking system but redistribute them.

3. Central Bank Operations

- Process: Central banks can inject or remove credits from the banking system.

- Examples: Open market operations, discount window lending

- Implications: These operations directly affect the overall supply of bank credits.

4. Credit Creation and Destruction

- Process: Banks create new credits when they make loans and destroy credits when loans are repaid.

- Implications: This process directly affects the money supply and can be seen as a form of credit transfer from potential to actual existence.

### Legal Implications of Credit Possession and Transfer

The possession and transfer of bank credits have significant legal implications, both for banks and their customers.

Key Legal Considerations:

1. Ownership Rights: Who legally owns the credits at each stage of a transfer?

2. Timing of Transfers: When exactly does legal possession change hands?

3. Disputes and Errors: How are disputes over credit transfers resolved?

4. Regulatory Compliance: How do banks ensure compliance with laws governing credit transfers?

Case Study: Wire Transfer Errors

Examining a case where a wire transfer was erroneously sent to the wrong recipient can illustrate the complex legal issues surrounding credit transfers:

- Scenario: Bank A mistakenly transfers $1 million to Account X instead of Account Y.

- Legal Questions:

- Does Bank A or the intended recipient have the right to reclaim the funds?

- What obligations does the unintended recipient have?

- How do banking regulations protect (or not protect) the parties involved?

### Practical Challenges in Credit Transfer

Despite the electronic nature of modern banking, credit transfers can still face practical challenges.

Common Issues:

1. Technical Failures: System outages or glitches can disrupt transfers.

2. Timing Mismatches: Different systems may process transfers at different speeds.

3. Cross-Border Complexities: International transfers involve multiple jurisdictions and currencies.

4. Fraud and Security: Electronic systems are vulnerable to cyber attacks and fraud.

### The Role of Blockchain and Cryptocurrencies

Emerging technologies are challenging traditional notions of credit possession and transfer.

Blockchain Technology:

- Offers a decentralized approach to recording and transferring value.

- Could potentially change how banks "possess" and transfer credits.

Cryptocurrencies and Central Bank Digital Currencies (CBDCs):

- Present new forms of digital value that blur the lines between traditional bank credits and other forms of money.

- May lead to new regulatory frameworks for credit possession and transfer.

### Regulatory Oversight of Credit Transfers

Regulators play a crucial role in overseeing how banks possess and transfer credits.

Key Regulatory Concerns:

1. Anti-Money Laundering (AML): Ensuring credits are not used for illegal purposes.

2. Know Your Customer (KYC): Verifying the identity of parties involved in credit transfers.

3. Capital Adequacy: Ensuring banks maintain sufficient capital relative to their credit activities.

4. Systemic Risk: Monitoring large credit transfers that could affect financial stability.

The possession and transfer of bank credits is a complex process that lies at the heart of modern banking operations. As we've seen, the electronic nature of today's financial system has transformed how we understand credit "possession," making it more a matter of authority and ability to manipulate digital records than physical holding.

The mechanisms for transferring credits are diverse and sophisticated, involving intricate networks of banks, clearing systems, and regulatory oversight. These processes come with significant legal implications and practical challenges, which banks must navigate carefully.

As technology continues to evolve, particularly with the advent of blockchain and digital currencies, the nature of credit possession and transfer is likely to undergo further transformations. Understanding these processes is crucial for anyone seeking to comprehend the workings of our financial system and the basis for banking transactions and contracts.

In the next chapter, we'll explore how banks ensure that their acquisition and use of credits comply with legal and regulatory requirements, building on the concepts we've discussed here.

# Chapter 6: Lawful Acquisition of Bank Credits

In our journey through the complex world of banking, we've explored the nature, creation, valuation, possession, and transfer of bank credits. Now, we turn our attention to a critical aspect that underpins the entire banking system: the lawful acquisition of bank credits. This chapter will delve into the regulatory framework governing banking operations, the processes banks must follow to acquire credits lawfully, and the consequences of failing to adhere to these standards.

### Regulatory Framework for Banking Operations

The banking industry is one of the most heavily regulated sectors of the economy, and for good reason. The stability of the financial system is crucial for economic health, and the lawful acquisition of bank credits is a key component of this stability.

Key Regulatory Bodies:

1. Central Banks: (e.g., Federal Reserve in the US, European Central Bank in the EU)

- Set monetary policy

- Supervise banks

- Act as lender of last resort

2. Financial Regulatory Agencies: (e.g., SEC, FDIC in the US, FCA in the UK)

- Enforce banking laws and regulations

- Protect consumers

- Ensure fair and efficient markets

3. International Organizations: (e.g., Bank for International Settlements, Financial Stability Board)

- Promote global financial stability

- Set international banking standards

Key Banking Regulations:

1. Basel Accords: International regulatory framework for banks
- Sets standards for capital requirements
- Addresses market liquidity risk
- Introduces stress testing requirements
2. Dodd-Frank Act (US): Implemented in response to the 2008 financial crisis
- Created the Consumer Financial Protection Bureau
- Introduced the Volcker Rule limiting speculative investments
3. Markets in Financial Instruments Directive (MiFID) (EU): Regulates investment services across the European Economic Area
- Aims to increase competition and consumer protection in investment services

### Lawful Means of Acquiring Bank Credits

Banks acquire credits through various means, all of which must comply with regulatory requirements.
1. Deposit Taking
- Process: Banks accept deposits from customers, which become liabilities on their balance sheets.
- Regulatory Considerations:
- Must comply with reserve requirements
- Subject to deposit insurance regulations
- Required to implement Know Your Customer (KYC) procedures
2. Borrowing from Other Banks or the Central Bank
- Process: Banks borrow from each other in the interbank market or from the central bank.
- Regulatory Considerations:
- Subject to interest rate limits
- Must maintain adequate collateral for central bank borrowing
- Borrowing activities are monitored for systemic risk
3. Issuing Securities
- Process: Banks raise funds by issuing bonds or other securities.
- Regulatory Considerations:

- Must comply with securities laws and disclosure requirements
- Subject to capital adequacy rules
- May require regulatory approval for certain types of securities

4. Credit Creation through Lending
- Process: Banks create new credits when they make loans.
- Regulatory Considerations:
- Must adhere to capital adequacy requirements
- Subject to lending limits and risk management regulations
- Required to implement credit risk assessment procedures

Anti-Money Laundering (AML) and Know Your Customer (KYC) Regulations

A crucial aspect of lawful credit acquisition is ensuring that the funds entering the banking system are from legitimate sources.

Key Components of AML/KYC Regulations:

1. Customer Identification: Verifying the identity of account holders and beneficial owners.

2. Transaction Monitoring: Identifying and reporting suspicious transactions.

3. Risk Assessment: Evaluating the money laundering risk associated with different customers and transactions.

4. Reporting: Filing Suspicious Activity Reports (SARs) with relevant authorities.

Case Study: HSBC Money Laundering Scandal

- In 2012, HSBC was fined $1.9 billion for failing to prevent money laundering by drug cartels.

- This case highlighted the importance of robust AML procedures in lawful credit acquisition.

**The Role of Technology in Lawful Credit Acquisition**

Advancements in technology are playing an increasingly important role in ensuring the lawful acquisition of bank credits.

Key Technological Tools:

1. Artificial Intelligence and Machine Learning: Used for transaction monitoring and fraud detection.

2. Blockchain: Potential applications in creating transparent and immutable transaction records.

3. Biometrics: Enhancing customer identification processes.

4. Big Data Analytics: Improving risk assessment and regulatory reporting capabilities.

## Consequences of Unlawful Credit Acquisition

Banks that fail to adhere to regulations regarding credit acquisition can face severe consequences.

Potential Penalties:

1. Financial Fines: Often running into billions of dollars for major violations.

2. Regulatory Sanctions: Including restrictions on certain banking activities.

3. Criminal Charges: For egregious violations, individuals may face criminal prosecution.

4. Reputational Damage: Can lead to loss of customers and business opportunities.

Case Study: Wells Fargo Account Fraud Scandal

- In 2016, Wells Fargo was fined $185 million for creating millions of fraudulent accounts.

- This case illustrates the severe consequences of unlawful practices in credit acquisition.

## Ethical Considerations in Credit Acquisition

Beyond legal compliance, banks must also consider ethical implications of their credit acquisition practices.

Key Ethical Issues:

1. Predatory Lending: Ensuring that credit is not extended on unfair or deceptive terms.

2. Financial Inclusion: Balancing risk management with the need to provide banking services to underserved communities.

3. Environmental and Social Responsibility: Considering the broader impacts of credit allocation decisions.

4. Transparency: Providing clear and understandable information to customers about banking products and services.

### International Aspects of Lawful Credit Acquisition

In an increasingly globalized financial system, banks must navigate complex international regulations.

**Key Challenges:**

1. Jurisdictional Differences: Dealing with varying regulatory requirements across countries.

2. Cross-Border Transactions: Ensuring compliance in international money transfers.

3. Extraterritorial Regulations: Adhering to laws that extend beyond national borders (e.g., US FATCA).

4. Global Systemic Risk: Managing credits in a way that doesn't contribute to global financial instability.

The lawful acquisition of bank credits is a complex process that requires careful navigation of a dense regulatory landscape. Banks must balance their need to acquire credits and conduct business with the imperative to comply with a myriad of laws and regulations designed to ensure financial stability, prevent criminal activity, and protect consumers.

As we've seen, the consequences of failing to acquire credits lawfully can be severe, ranging from hefty fines to criminal charges and lasting reputational damage. At the same time, evolving technologies are providing new tools for compliance while also presenting new challenges.

Understanding these processes and requirements is crucial not only for banking professionals but also for customers, investors, and anyone seeking to comprehend the foundations of our financial system. As regulations continue to evolve in response to new challenges and technologies, the landscape of lawful credit acquisition will undoubtedly continue to change, requiring ongoing vigilance and adaptation from all stakeholders in the financial system.

In the next chapter, we'll explore how these regulatory requirements and lawful acquisition processes impact the establishment and enforcement of banking contracts.

# Chapter 7: The Burden of Proof in Banking Disputes

In our exploration of banking practices, contracts, and regulations, we now turn to a critical aspect of financial disputes: the burden of proof. When disagreements arise between banks and their customers, or when regulatory bodies investigate banking practices, the question of who must prove what becomes paramount. This chapter will delve into the legal standards for proving the existence of a contract, the role of documentary evidence in banking transactions, and the complexities introduced by modern electronic banking systems.

Legal Standards for Proving the Existence of a Contract

In banking disputes, the existence and terms of a contract are often at the heart of the matter. The legal standard for proving a contract exists can vary depending on the jurisdiction and the nature of the agreement.

### Elements of a Valid Contract

Typically, to prove the existence of a contract, the following elements must be demonstrated:

1. Offer: One party made a clear proposal.

2. Acceptance: The other party agreed to the terms of the offer.

3. Consideration: Something of value was exchanged.

4. Capacity: Both parties were legally able to enter into the contract.

5. Intention: Both parties intended to create a legally binding agreement.

### Burden of Proof in Contract Disputes

- Civil Cases: The standard is usually "preponderance of the evidence" (more likely than not).

- Criminal Cases: The standard is "beyond a reasonable doubt" (much higher threshold).

Case Study: Smith v. FirstBank (2019)

- Customer claimed no agreement to overdraft fees

- Bank produced signed account agreement and electronic records of customer's acknowledgment

- Court ruled in favor of the bank, illustrating the importance of documentary evidence

**Documentary Evidence in Banking Transactions**

Banks rely heavily on documentation to prove the existence and terms of agreements with customers.

**Types of Documentary Evidence:**

1. Account Agreements: Signed documents outlining terms and conditions.

2. Loan Documents: Contracts specifying loan terms, interest rates, and repayment schedules.

3. Electronic Acknowledgments: Records of customers agreeing to terms online.

4. Transaction Records: Detailed logs of account activity and transfers.

5. Correspondence: Emails, letters, and recorded phone calls discussing account details.

Importance of Record Keeping

- Banks are required by law to maintain certain records for specified periods.

- Failure to produce required documentation can severely weaken a bank's position in disputes.

**Challenges in Documentary Evidence**

- Volume of Data: Banks handle millions of transactions, making comprehensive record-keeping challenging.

- Data Integrity: Ensuring the accuracy and tamper-proof nature of electronic records.

- Privacy Concerns: Balancing record-keeping with customer privacy rights.

The Role of Electronic Records and Digital Signatures

As banking has moved increasingly online, electronic records and digital signatures have become crucial in proving the existence and terms of agreements.

Legal Recognition of Electronic Signatures

- Many jurisdictions have laws recognizing the validity of electronic signatures (e.g., E-SIGN Act in the US, eIDAS Regulation in the EU).

**Challenges with Electronic Evidence**

1. Authentication: Proving the authenticity of electronic records.

2. Alteration Detection: Demonstrating that records haven't been tampered with.

3. Long-term Preservation: Ensuring records remain accessible and verifiable over time.

Case Study: Johnson v. CityBank (2021)

- Customer disputed online loan application

- Bank provided IP address logs, click-through records, and digital signature data

- Court accepted electronic evidence as proof of agreement

Regulatory Requirements for Proof in Banking

Regulatory bodies often set specific requirements for what banks must be able to prove and how.

**Key Regulatory Standards:**

1. Know Your Customer (KYC): Banks must prove they've verified customer identities.

2. Anti-Money Laundering (AML): Evidence of due diligence in monitoring and reporting suspicious activities.

3. Fair Lending Laws: Proof of non-discriminatory lending practices.

4. Consumer Protection Regulations: Evidence of compliance with disclosure requirements and fair practices.

Consequences of Failing to Meet Burden of Proof

- Regulatory fines and penalties

- Forced changes to banking practices

- Reputational damage

Shifting Burdens of Proof

In some cases, the burden of proof may shift between parties during a dispute.

Examples of Shifting Burden:

1. Unauthorized Transactions: Initially on the bank to prove authorization, may shift to customer if bank shows security measures were in place.

2. Discriminatory Lending: Initially on the plaintiff to show disparity, may shift to bank to prove non-discriminatory reasons.

Factors Influencing Burden Shifts:

- Nature of the allegation

- Statutory requirements

- Access to relevant information

The Impact of Technology on the Burden of Proof

Advancements in technology are changing how proof is established in banking disputes.

Blockchain and Distributed Ledger Technology

- Potential to provide immutable, transparent transaction records

- Challenges in legal recognition and interpretation of blockchain data

Artificial Intelligence and Machine Learning

- Used for pattern recognition in fraud detection

- Raises questions about explainability and bias in decision-making processes

Big Data Analytics

- Enables more comprehensive transaction monitoring

- Challenges in data privacy and relevance of vast data sets

Challenges in Meeting the Burden of Proof

Banks face several challenges in meeting their burden of proof in disputes.

Common Challenges:

1. Data Overload: Managing and effectively using vast amounts of transaction data.

2. Technological Complexity: Explaining technical processes to non-technical judges and juries.

3. Evolving Regulatory Landscape: Keeping up with changing requirements for evidence and proof.

4. Cross-Border Issues: Dealing with different legal standards across jurisdictions.

Strategies for Addressing Challenges:

1. Robust Documentation Practices: Implementing comprehensive, consistent record-keeping.

2. Regular Audits: Conducting internal reviews to ensure compliance and identify gaps.

3. Staff Training: Ensuring employees understand the importance of documentation and regulatory compliance.

4. Technology Investment: Implementing systems to better manage and analyze data.

The Role of Expert Witnesses

In complex banking disputes, expert witnesses often play a crucial role in helping courts understand technical evidence.

Types of Expert Witnesses in Banking Cases:

1. Forensic Accountants: Analyze financial records and trace transactions.

2. IT Specialists: Explain electronic systems and data security measures.

3. Banking Regulation Experts: Provide context on industry standards and regulatory requirements.

Challenges with Expert Testimony:

- Ensuring impartiality

- Translating complex concepts for non-expert audiences
- Dealing with conflicting expert opinions

The burden of proof in banking disputes is a complex and evolving area of law. As we've seen, banks must navigate a challenging landscape of regulatory requirements, technological advancements, and changing legal standards. The ability to prove the existence and terms of contracts, the legitimacy of transactions, and compliance with regulations is crucial for banks to maintain their legal standing and public trust.

At the same time, customers and regulators are increasingly empowered to challenge banks, shifting the dynamics of who must prove what in various situations. This evolving landscape underscores the importance of robust documentation practices, technological innovation, and a thorough understanding of legal and regulatory requirements.

As banking continues to evolve with new technologies and business models, the nature of proof in banking disputes will likely continue to change. Banks, customers, regulators, and legal professionals must stay informed and adaptable to navigate this complex terrain effectively.

In the next chapter, we'll explore how the concepts of proof and evidence we've discussed here apply specifically to the establishment of consideration in banking contracts, a crucial element in determining their validity and enforceability.

# Chapter 8: Consideration and Exchange in Banking Contracts

Defining "Exchange" in the Context of Banking

In the realm of banking, the concept of "exchange" is fundamental to understanding the nature of financial transactions. An exchange in banking refers to the transfer of value between two or more parties, where one party provides something of value—such as money, goods, services, or financial instruments—and the other party provides a reciprocal value in return. This reciprocal arrangement forms the basis of all banking transactions, from simple deposits and withdrawals to complex loan agreements and derivatives trading.

Exchange in banking is not limited to tangible assets like currency or commodities; it also encompasses intangible assets, including credit, promises to pay, and the transfer of rights and obligations. For example, when a customer deposits money into a bank account, they are effectively exchanging their cash for the bank's promise to repay that amount upon demand, plus any agreed-upon interest. Similarly, when a bank issues a loan, it exchanges the loan amount with the borrower's commitment to repay the principal along with interest over a specified period.

The banking system operates on the principle of trust and the expectation that each party will fulfill their part of the exchange. This trust is often formalized through written contracts, which outline the terms and conditions of the exchange, ensuring that both parties are legally bound to uphold their obligations.

### How Consideration is Established in Financial Transactions

Consideration is a core component of any valid contract, including those within the banking sector. In legal terms, consideration refers to something of value that is given by one party to another as part of a contractual agreement. It is the glue that binds a contract, making it enforceable in a court of law. For a contract to be valid, there must be an offer, acceptance, and consideration. In banking, consideration is typically established through the mutual exchange of promises or the transfer of something of value.

In a banking contract, consideration can take various forms:

1. Monetary Consideration: This is the most straightforward form of consideration in banking transactions. For example, when a customer takes out a loan, the bank provides the loan amount as consideration. In return, the borrower promises to repay the loan amount along with interest, which constitutes the bank's consideration. The interest paid over time compensates the bank for the opportunity cost of lending the money and the risk associated with the loan.

2. Service Consideration: Consideration can also be in the form of services rendered. For instance, a bank may provide investment advisory services to a client. The consideration from the bank's side is the expertise and advice offered, while the client's consideration is the fees paid for those services.

3. Promise-Based Consideration: Often in banking, consideration involves a promise to act or refrain from acting in a certain way. For example, when opening a savings account, the bank promises to pay interest on the deposited funds, while the depositor agrees to maintain a certain balance or adhere to specific account terms.

4. Forbearance as Consideration: Forbearance refers to the act of refraining from enforcing a right or claim. In banking, forbearance can be a form of consideration. For instance, if a bank agrees not to demand immediate repayment of a delinquent loan, this act of forbearance can be considered consideration, especially if the borrower agrees to certain conditions in exchange, such as paying a higher interest rate or providing additional collateral.

The establishment of consideration is critical because it ensures that both parties have a stake in the contract. Without consideration, a contract could be deemed a mere gift or promise, lacking the necessary elements to be legally binding. In the context of banking, consideration underpins the trust and reciprocity that are essential for financial stability and the smooth operation of the banking system.

Challenging the Validity of a Transaction Based on Lack of Consideration

While consideration is a key element in the formation of a valid contract, there are instances where the validity of a banking transaction may be challenged due to a lack of consideration. In legal disputes, the absence of consideration can be grounds for declaring a contract void or unenforceable.

1. Failure of Consideration: This occurs when one party fails to provide the promised consideration, thereby undermining the contract's validity. For example, if a bank fails to deliver the loan amount as agreed upon in the loan contract, the borrower may challenge the validity of the contract due to the bank's failure to provide the consideration. Similarly, if a borrower defaults on loan repayments, the bank could argue that the borrower's failure to provide the promised repayment constitutes a failure of consideration.

2. Insufficient Consideration: In some cases, the consideration provided by one party may be deemed insufficient to support a binding contract. This does not necessarily mean that the consideration has to be of equal value, but it must be legally sufficient. For example, if a bank agrees to provide a loan but the borrower offers an unrealistic or nominal interest rate as consideration, the bank could argue that the consideration is insufficient to make the contract enforceable.

3. Past Consideration: Consideration must be contemporaneous with the contract's formation; past actions or services do not constitute valid consideration. In banking, this means that any services or actions taken before the formal agreement of a contract cannot be used as consideration for that contract. For example, if a client claims that previous advisory services provided by a bank should serve as consideration for a new loan agreement, this argument would likely fail since those services were not part of the new contract's terms.

4. Illegality of Consideration: If the consideration involves illegal actions or agreements, the contract may be declared void. In banking, any contract that involves illegal consideration, such as money laundering or financing illicit activities, would not be enforceable. Banks are subject to strict regulatory frameworks to prevent such transactions, and any involvement in illegal consideration could lead to severe legal repercussions.

5. Illusory Consideration: A promise that is vague or lacks specificity may be considered illusory, rendering the contract unenforceable. In banking, if a promise is made that is so uncertain or open-ended that it does not impose a real obligation, it could be considered illusory. For example, if a bank agrees to "consider" providing a loan without specifying terms or amounts, this promise may not constitute valid consideration.

Challenging the validity of a banking transaction based on lack of consideration can have significant implications. It not only affects the parties directly involved but also has broader implications for the trust and reliability of the banking system. As such, banks must ensure that all contracts are supported by adequate and lawful consideration to maintain their enforceability and uphold the integrity of financial transactions.

In conclusion, understanding the concepts of exchange and consideration in banking contracts is crucial for ensuring that financial transactions are legally sound and enforceable. By clearly defining exchange, establishing consideration, and recognizing the grounds on which a transaction can be challenged for lack of consideration, banks and their clients can better navigate the complexities of contractual agreements, promoting transparency, trust, and stability in the financial system.

# Chapter 9: Establishing Valid Contracts in Banking

A banking contract forms the backbone of many financial transactions, providing a legal framework that defines the rights and obligations of the parties involved. Whether it's opening a savings account, taking out a mortgage, or entering into a complex derivative transaction, the validity of these contracts is essential to the functioning of the financial system. This chapter explores the key elements that establish a valid banking contract, the common pitfalls and misunderstandings that can arise, and the strategies consumers can use to protect their interests.

**Key Elements That Prove the Existence of a Banking Contract**

For any contract to be valid and enforceable, including those in the banking sector, certain fundamental elements must be present. These elements ensure that all parties involved are legally bound to uphold their obligations under the contract. The key elements that prove the existence of a banking contract are as follows:

1. Offer: The offer is a proposal by one party to enter into an agreement with another party. In the context of banking, an offer can take many forms, such as a bank offering a loan product, a credit card, or an investment service. The offer must be clear and specific, outlining the terms of the agreement, including the amount of money involved, the interest rate, the repayment schedule, and any other relevant conditions. An offer must be communicated to the other party, who then has the option to accept or decline it.

2. Acceptance: Acceptance is the unequivocal agreement to the terms of the offer by the party receiving it. In banking, acceptance occurs when a customer signs a loan agreement, agrees to the terms of a savings account, or consents to the conditions of a credit card application. Acceptance must mirror the offer exactly; any changes or conditions would constitute a counteroffer, not an acceptance. Once acceptance is

communicated, a contract is formed, provided all other elements of a valid contract are present.

3. Consideration: As discussed in the previous chapter, consideration is something of value exchanged between the parties involved. In banking, consideration is often monetary but can also involve the provision of services or the promise to perform certain actions. For example, in a loan agreement, the bank provides funds to the borrower, and the borrower agrees to repay the principal plus interest. This mutual exchange of value is what makes the contract legally binding.

4. Intention to Create Legal Relations: For a contract to be valid, both parties must have the intention to enter into a legally binding agreement. In the banking sector, this intention is typically implicit, given the nature of financial transactions and the formality with which they are conducted. However, it must be clear that both parties understand the contract as a legal document with enforceable obligations. Casual agreements or vague promises are not considered contracts, as they lack this intention.

5. Capacity: Capacity refers to the legal ability of the parties to enter into a contract. In banking, this means that both the bank and the customer must have the legal standing to engage in the agreement. Individuals must be of legal age and sound mind, while corporations must have the authority to enter into contracts. If a party lacks capacity, the contract may be voidable or entirely void.

6. Legality of Purpose: The purpose of the contract must be legal and not against public policy. Banking contracts must comply with applicable laws and regulations. Any agreement involving illegal activities, such as money laundering or financing illicit trade, would be void and unenforceable. Banks are required to conduct due diligence to ensure that their contracts are for legitimate purposes and comply with legal standards.

7. Certainty and Clarity of Terms: The terms of a banking contract must be clear and specific to avoid ambiguity and misunderstanding. All

essential aspects of the agreement, such as interest rates, fees, repayment schedules, and penalties, should be explicitly stated. Any vagueness or ambiguity in the terms can lead to disputes and may render the contract unenforceable.

**Common Pitfalls and Misunderstandings in Banking Agreements**
Despite the formal nature of banking contracts, several common pitfalls and misunderstandings can arise, potentially leading to disputes or rendering a contract invalid. Understanding these pitfalls can help both banks and customers avoid legal challenges and ensure that their agreements are enforceable.

1. Ambiguous Terms: One of the most common pitfalls in banking agreements is the use of ambiguous terms or language. Vague or unclear terms can lead to different interpretations of the contract's obligations, which can result in disputes. For example, if a loan agreement does not clearly define the conditions under which the interest rate may change, it could lead to misunderstandings and conflicts between the bank and the borrower.

2. Failure to Fully Disclose Terms: Full disclosure is critical in banking contracts to ensure that all parties understand their rights and obligations. A common misunderstanding occurs when a bank fails to disclose all the terms of a contract, such as hidden fees, penalties, or changes in interest rates. This lack of transparency can lead to claims of misrepresentation or fraud, potentially invalidating the contract.

3. Assuming Oral Agreements Are Binding: While oral agreements can sometimes constitute valid contracts, banking transactions typically require written documentation due to the complexity and financial stakes involved. Relying on oral agreements or informal promises can lead to significant misunderstandings, as these are difficult to prove in court. Banks and customers should ensure that all agreements are documented in writing and signed by both parties.

4. Uninformed Consent: For a contract to be valid, all parties must provide informed consent, meaning they understand the contract's terms and conditions. In some cases, customers may sign agreements without fully understanding the implications, such as the risks associated with a financial product or the long-term costs of a loan. This lack of understanding can lead to disputes and claims that the contract was entered into under duress or without adequate information.

5. Failure to Update Terms: Banking contracts may need to be updated periodically to reflect changes in regulations, market conditions, or the parties' circumstances. Failure to update the terms of a contract can lead to misunderstandings and disputes, particularly if one party assumes the old terms still apply. Banks should ensure that all contract amendments are properly documented and communicated to the customer.

6. Breach of Contractual Obligations: A breach occurs when one party fails to fulfill its obligations under the contract. In banking, breaches can happen if a customer fails to make loan payments or if a bank does not provide services as agreed. Misunderstandings about what constitutes a breach can lead to disputes and legal action.

### Strategies for Consumers to Protect Their Interests

Consumers have a vested interest in ensuring that their banking contracts are valid, clear, and enforceable. By taking proactive steps, they can protect their interests and avoid potential pitfalls in their financial agreements.

1. Thoroughly Read and Understand All Contracts: Consumers should carefully read and understand every contract before signing. This includes reviewing all terms, conditions, fees, and obligations. If any part of the contract is unclear, consumers should seek clarification from the bank or a legal professional. Understanding the full scope of the agreement helps prevent misunderstandings and disputes.

2. Ask Questions and Seek Clarification: If any terms or conditions in a banking contract are confusing or ambiguous, consumers should not

hesitate to ask questions. Banks have a duty to provide clear explanations of their products and services. Consumers should ensure they fully understand the contract and its implications before agreeing to it.

3. Request Written Documentation: To avoid misunderstandings and ensure enforceability, consumers should request written documentation of all agreements and transactions. This includes any amendments or changes to the original contract. Written contracts provide clear evidence of the terms agreed upon and can be crucial in resolving disputes.

4. Be Aware of Consumer Rights and Protections: Consumers should be aware of their rights under applicable consumer protection laws. These laws are designed to prevent unfair practices and ensure transparency in banking transactions. Knowing these rights can help consumers recognize when a contract may be unfair or when a bank may not be acting in good faith.

5. Seek Professional Advice: In complex financial transactions or when dealing with unfamiliar banking products, consumers may benefit from seeking advice from a financial advisor or attorney. These professionals can provide valuable insights and help consumers understand the risks and benefits associated with different banking contracts.

6. Regularly Review and Monitor Agreements: Consumers should regularly review their banking agreements to ensure they remain valid and reflect their current circumstances. This is particularly important for long-term contracts, such as mortgages or investment products, which may be affected by changes in market conditions or regulations. Regular monitoring can help consumers identify any discrepancies or issues that need to be addressed.

7. Negotiate Terms When Possible: While many banking contracts are standard form contracts with non-negotiable terms, there may be some room for negotiation, especially for large transactions or long-term relationships. Consumers should not hesitate to negotiate terms that

are unfavorable or request modifications that better suit their needs. Effective negotiation can lead to more favorable terms and reduce the risk of future disputes.

In conclusion, establishing valid contracts in banking requires a clear understanding of the fundamental elements that constitute a legally binding agreement. By being aware of the common pitfalls and misunderstandings that can arise, consumers can take proactive steps to protect their interests and ensure that their banking contracts are fair, transparent, and enforceable. Banks, in turn, must ensure that their contracts are clear, compliant with legal standards, and reflect the mutual intentions of the parties involved, fostering trust and stability in the financial system.

# Chapter 10: Legal Claims and Entitlements in Banking Disputes

Banking disputes arise when conflicts occur between a bank and its customers over the terms, conditions, or performance of banking contracts. Understanding the nature of legal claims and entitlements in these disputes is essential for both banks and consumers. This chapter delves into the types of claims banks can make against customers, the defenses available against improper banking claims, and the rights and protections afforded to consumers in banking disputes.

**Types of Claims Banks Can Make Against Customers**

In the course of their operations, banks may need to make various claims against customers due to breaches of contract or non-compliance with agreed terms. Here are some of the common types of claims banks can make:

1. Breach of Contract: A breach of contract occurs when a customer fails to fulfill their obligations under a banking agreement. Common breaches in banking include missed loan payments, overdrawing accounts beyond agreed limits, and failing to maintain required balances. When a breach occurs, the bank may file a claim seeking to recover the outstanding amount, plus any interest, penalties, or fees specified in the contract.

2. Recovery of Debt: When a customer defaults on a loan or credit card payment, the bank can initiate legal proceedings to recover the debt. This claim typically includes the principal amount owed, accrued interest, late fees, and any legal costs incurred by the bank in pursuing the debt. In some cases, banks may also seek a judgment allowing them to garnish wages or seize assets to satisfy the debt.

3. Fraudulent Misrepresentation: If a customer provides false information or intentionally conceals relevant details when entering into a banking agreement, the bank may have grounds to claim fraudulent

misrepresentation. For example, providing inaccurate income information on a loan application could lead to a claim if the bank relied on that information in making its decision. Banks can seek damages for any losses suffered due to the customer's misrepresentation.

4. Conversion: Conversion occurs when a customer wrongfully takes or retains possession of the bank's property. In banking, this could involve unauthorized withdrawals or transfers from accounts, or the misuse of funds meant for specific purposes (e.g., using business loan funds for personal expenses). Banks can claim conversion to recover the misappropriated funds and may seek punitive damages in cases of intentional misconduct.

5. Enforcement of Security Interests: When banks lend money, they often require collateral or security to protect against the risk of default. If a customer defaults on a secured loan, the bank can make a claim to enforce its security interest. This typically involves seizing and selling the collateral (such as a home, vehicle, or other asset) to recover the outstanding debt.

6. Unjust Enrichment: This claim arises when a customer benefits unfairly at the expense of the bank. In the context of banking, unjust enrichment could occur if a customer mistakenly receives funds they are not entitled to, such as an overpayment or an erroneous credit to their account. The bank can file a claim to recover the funds and ensure that the customer does not retain the undeserved benefit.

7. Statutory Claims: In addition to contractual claims, banks may also pursue statutory claims under applicable laws and regulations. For instance, banks may seek to enforce anti-money laundering regulations, consumer protection laws, or tax reporting requirements. Non-compliance with these regulations can lead to claims against customers for penalties, fines, or corrective actions.

### Defenses Against Improper Banking Claims

While banks have the right to make claims against customers, not all claims are justified or legally valid. Customers have several defenses they can use to challenge improper banking claims:

1. Lack of Contractual Basis: One of the primary defenses against a bank's claim is the argument that there is no valid contract in place. If a customer can demonstrate that a contract was never formed (due to lack of offer, acceptance, consideration, or capacity), or if the contract is void due to illegality or fraud, they may successfully defend against the bank's claim.

2. Performance of Obligations: A customer may defend against a claim by proving that they have fulfilled their contractual obligations. For example, if a bank alleges that a customer defaulted on a loan, the customer can present evidence of payments made on time and in full. Documentation such as bank statements, payment receipts, or correspondence with the bank can be crucial in establishing performance.

3. Misrepresentation or Fraud by the Bank: If a bank made false representations or withheld critical information when forming the contract, the customer might have a defense based on misrepresentation or fraud. For instance, if a bank misled a customer about the terms of a loan or the risks associated with an investment, the customer could argue that the contract is voidable and that the bank's claim should be dismissed.

4. Breach of Contract by the Bank: Customers can counter a bank's claim by demonstrating that the bank itself breached the contract. For example, if a bank failed to disburse loan funds as agreed, did not provide agreed-upon services, or violated the terms of a deposit agreement, the customer might argue that the bank's breach excused their non-performance.

5. Duress or Undue Influence: Contracts obtained under duress or undue influence are not enforceable. If a customer can show that they were coerced into signing a contract or that the bank took advantage of

their position, they may successfully defend against a claim. This defense is particularly relevant in cases where customers felt pressured into accepting unfavorable terms.

6. Unconscionability: A contract may be deemed unconscionable if it is so one-sided or oppressive that it shocks the conscience. If a customer can prove that a banking contract is unconscionable—such as containing exorbitant fees or interest rates, or imposing unduly harsh penalties—they may have a valid defense against the bank's claim.

7. Estoppel: Estoppel is a legal principle that prevents a party from going back on a promise or representation if the other party has relied on it to their detriment. In banking disputes, a customer could argue estoppel if the bank made a promise (such as waiving a fee or extending a payment deadline) and the customer acted in reliance on that promise.

8. Statute of Limitations: Most legal claims are subject to a statute of limitations, which sets a time limit on when a claim can be filed. If a bank waits too long to bring a claim against a customer, the customer may be able to use the statute of limitations as a defense, effectively barring the bank from pursuing the claim.

### Consumer Rights and Protections in Banking Disputes

Consumers have a range of rights and protections designed to ensure fair treatment in banking disputes. These rights help balance the power dynamic between banks and individual customers, providing avenues for redress and holding banks accountable for their actions.

1. Right to Fair Treatment: Consumers have the right to be treated fairly by their banks, which includes transparent communication, ethical behavior, and respect for privacy. Banks are obligated to provide clear and accurate information about their products and services and must not engage in deceptive or unfair practices.

2. Right to Access Information: Under various consumer protection laws, customers have the right to access information related to their accounts, transactions, and any disputes with the bank. This includes receiving copies of contracts, statements, and any communications

related to the dispute. Access to information helps customers understand their rights and build a case if needed.

3. Right to Challenge and Dispute: Consumers have the right to challenge and dispute any charges, fees, or actions taken by the bank that they believe are incorrect or unfair. This includes unauthorized transactions, incorrect fees, or errors in account management. Most banks have formal dispute resolution procedures, and customers should use these processes to resolve issues.

4. Protection Against Unauthorized Transactions: Customers are protected against unauthorized transactions on their accounts, such as fraudulent withdrawals, transfers, or charges. In many jurisdictions, banks are required to investigate and, if necessary, reimburse customers for losses due to unauthorized transactions, provided the customer reports the issue promptly.

5. Right to Privacy: Consumers have the right to privacy regarding their personal and financial information. Banks are required to protect this information and must obtain customer consent before sharing it with third parties, except as required by law. If a bank breaches this duty of confidentiality, the customer may have grounds for a legal claim.

6. Protection Under Consumer Protection Laws: Numerous consumer protection laws safeguard customers' rights in banking transactions. For example, the Truth in Lending Act (TILA) in the United States requires lenders to disclose the terms and costs of credit, while the Fair Credit Reporting Act (FCRA) ensures the accuracy and privacy of credit report information. Other laws, like the Equal Credit Opportunity Act (ECOA), prohibit discrimination in lending based on race, gender, age, or other protected characteristics.

7. Right to Legal Representation: In any dispute with a bank, customers have the right to seek legal representation. An attorney can provide valuable advice, negotiate with the bank on the customer's behalf, and represent the customer in court if necessary. Legal

representation is particularly important in complex disputes or when significant financial interests are at stake.

8. Right to Alternative Dispute Resolution (ADR): Many banking contracts include clauses that require disputes to be resolved through alternative dispute resolution methods, such as mediation or arbitration, rather than through litigation. ADR can be a faster and less expensive way to resolve disputes. Consumers have the right to request ADR if it is included in their agreement or if both parties agree to it.

9. Regulatory and Ombudsman Support: In many jurisdictions, consumers have access to regulatory bodies or ombudsman services that oversee the banking sector and handle complaints. These organizations provide an additional layer of protection by investigating complaints, resolving disputes, and ensuring that banks comply with regulations.

In conclusion, legal claims and entitlements in banking disputes are multifaceted, encompassing a wide range of potential conflicts between banks and customers. While banks have the right to make claims against customers, it is crucial for consumers to understand their defenses against improper claims and their rights and protections in these disputes. By being informed and proactive, consumers can navigate banking disputes effectively, ensuring that their rights are upheld and their financial interests protected. Banks, on the other hand, must adhere to legal standards and act in good faith to maintain trust and avoid disputes that could harm their reputation and customer relationships.

In the complex world of banking and finance, understanding the intricacies of banking contracts and consumer protections is more important than ever. As technology advances and the landscape of financial services evolves, consumers need to be equipped with the knowledge to navigate this environment confidently. This chapter emphasizes the importance of empowering oneself through financial literacy, explores the future of banking contracts and consumer protection, and provides resources for further learning and legal assistance.

Empowering Yourself Through Financial Literacy

Financial literacy is the cornerstone of sound financial decision-making and consumer empowerment. It involves understanding how money works, making informed decisions about financial products, and knowing your rights and responsibilities in financial transactions. Here are some key aspects of financial literacy that are particularly relevant to banking:

1. Understanding Financial Products and Services: Being financially literate means understanding the range of financial products and services available, from basic checking and savings accounts to more complex instruments like mortgages, credit cards, and investment accounts. By knowing how these products work, including their costs, benefits, and risks, consumers can make choices that align with their financial goals and avoid products that may not suit their needs.

2. Knowing Your Rights and Responsibilities: Financial literacy also includes an understanding of consumer rights and responsibilities. This knowledge empowers consumers to protect themselves against unfair practices, such as hidden fees, misleading terms, or unauthorized transactions. Being aware of your rights allows you to hold financial institutions accountable and seek redress when necessary.

3. Building Confidence in Financial Decision-Making: A solid foundation in financial literacy helps build confidence when making financial decisions. It enables consumers to negotiate better terms, recognize potentially harmful contracts, and understand the implications of their financial choices. Confidence in financial matters is critical to managing your finances effectively and achieving long-term financial stability.

4. Preparing for the Future: Financial literacy is not just about managing your current finances; it's also about preparing for the future. This includes planning for major life events, such as buying a home, saving for retirement, or funding education, as well as understanding how to navigate financial challenges like debt, unemployment, or

economic downturns. By being financially literate, you are better equipped to handle whatever the future brings.

## The Future of Banking Contracts and Consumer Protection

As we look to the future, several trends are likely to shape the landscape of banking contracts and consumer protection. These developments will have significant implications for both financial institutions and consumers:

1. Digital Transformation and Innovation: The banking sector is undergoing rapid digital transformation, driven by technological advancements and changing consumer expectations. Online banking, mobile apps, and digital wallets are becoming the norm, and financial technology (fintech) companies are challenging traditional banks with innovative products and services. While these developments offer greater convenience and accessibility, they also present new risks and challenges related to data privacy, cybersecurity, and the enforceability of digital contracts.

2. Increased Regulation and Oversight: In response to these changes, regulatory bodies around the world are enhancing their oversight of the banking sector. New regulations are being introduced to address issues like data protection, cybersecurity, anti-money laundering, and consumer rights in the digital age. These regulations aim to protect consumers from emerging risks while ensuring that financial institutions operate transparently and ethically.

3. Greater Focus on Consumer Education: As financial products become more complex and diverse, there is a growing recognition of the need for consumer education. Governments, regulatory bodies, and financial institutions are increasingly investing in financial literacy programs to help consumers understand their rights, make informed choices, and avoid falling victim to fraud or predatory practices. This trend is likely to continue as the financial landscape evolves.

4. Emergence of Smart Contracts and Blockchain Technology: Blockchain technology and smart contracts are transforming the way financial transactions are conducted and recorded. Smart contracts are self-executing contracts with the terms directly written into code, allowing for automatic enforcement and reducing the need for intermediaries. While this technology has the potential to increase efficiency and transparency, it also raises questions about regulation, security, and the protection of consumer rights.

5. Strengthening Consumer Protections: As part of the broader trend towards increased regulation, there is a growing emphasis on strengthening consumer protections. This includes introducing more robust mechanisms for dispute resolution, enhancing transparency in financial transactions, and ensuring that financial institutions act in the best interests of their customers. As consumer protections evolve, it will be important for consumers to stay informed about their rights and the resources available to them.

### Resources for Further Learning and Legal Assistance

To navigate the complexities of banking and finance effectively, consumers should take advantage of the many resources available for further learning and legal assistance. Here are some key resources to consider:

1. Online Financial Literacy Courses: Numerous online platforms offer free or low-cost courses on personal finance, banking, and investment. Websites like Coursera, Khan Academy, and Udemy provide courses that cover a wide range of topics, from basic budgeting and saving to more advanced subjects like investing and financial planning.

2. Government and Regulatory Websites: Many government agencies and regulatory bodies offer valuable information and resources on consumer rights, financial regulations, and banking practices. For example, the Consumer Financial Protection Bureau (CFPB) in the United States and the Financial Conduct Authority (FCA) in the United Kingdom provide guides, tools, and educational materials to

help consumers understand their rights and make informed financial decisions.

3. Nonprofit Organizations and Advocacy Groups: Nonprofit organizations and advocacy groups often provide free resources, workshops, and counseling on financial literacy and consumer rights. Groups like the National Foundation for Credit Counseling (NFCC), the Consumer Federation of America (CFA), and the Financial Consumer Agency of Canada (FCAC) offer valuable support to consumers dealing with financial challenges.

4. Legal Aid Services: For those who need legal assistance in banking disputes or other financial matters, legal aid services can be a valuable resource. Legal aid organizations provide free or low-cost legal representation to individuals who cannot afford private attorneys. In many jurisdictions, legal aid services are available to help consumers resolve disputes with financial institutions, negotiate settlements, or navigate the court system.

5. Financial Advisors and Counselors: Consulting a financial advisor or counselor can provide personalized guidance on managing your finances, understanding complex financial products, and planning for the future. Certified financial planners (CFPs) and accredited financial counselors (AFCs) are professionals who can help you make informed decisions and develop strategies to achieve your financial goals.

6. Libraries and Community Centers: Public libraries and community centers often host workshops, seminars, and events on financial literacy and consumer rights. These events are usually free to attend and provide an opportunity to learn from experts, ask questions, and connect with others in your community who are interested in financial education.

7. Consumer Protection Hotlines and Ombudsman Services: In many countries, consumer protection agencies and ombudsman services offer hotlines or online portals where consumers can get advice, file complaints, and seek assistance with financial disputes. These services are

designed to help consumers resolve issues quickly and efficiently without the need for costly litigation.

8. Financial Blogs and Podcasts: There are countless blogs and podcasts dedicated to personal finance, banking, and consumer rights. These resources offer a wealth of information and insights on a wide range of topics, from managing debt and building credit to understanding banking regulations and protecting yourself from fraud. Popular financial blogs and podcasts include The Simple Dollar, NerdWallet, and The Dave Ramsey Show.

In conclusion, navigating the world of banking and finance requires a combination of knowledge, vigilance, and proactive engagement. By empowering yourself through financial literacy, staying informed about the evolving landscape of banking contracts and consumer protections, and leveraging the resources available for further learning and legal assistance, you can make sound financial decisions and protect your interests. As the financial industry continues to evolve, staying educated and aware of your rights will be essential to achieving financial stability and success.

# Glossary

**Anti-Money Laundering (AML)**

Regulations and procedures designed to prevent criminals from disguising illegally obtained funds as legitimate income. AML policies are critical for banks to identify and report suspicious activities that may indicate money laundering.

**Banking Contracts**

Agreements between a bank and its customers that outline the terms and conditions of financial transactions, including loans, credit facilities, and deposit accounts. These contracts must be legally binding and enforceable to protect the interests of both parties.

**Bank Credits**

Financial resources that a bank extends to a customer, often in the form of loans or lines of credit. Bank credits are a central part of banking operations and can be categorized into various types, such as secured and unsecured credit, revolving credit, and term loans.

**Consideration**

A fundamental element of a valid contract, representing something of value exchanged between parties. In banking, consideration typically involves the promise to repay a loan with interest or the maintenance of a certain account balance.

**Consumer Protection**

Laws and regulations designed to safeguard consumers from unfair, deceptive, or abusive practices by financial institutions. Consumer protection laws ensure transparency, fairness, and accountability in financial transactions.

**Digital Signatures**

Electronic signatures that verify the identity of the signer and the integrity of the signed document. Digital signatures are commonly used in banking to authenticate contracts and transactions in a secure and legally binding manner.

**Electronic Records**

Digital documentation of financial transactions and agreements, including emails, online statements, and electronic contracts. Electronic records are increasingly used as evidence in banking disputes due to their accessibility and reliability.

**Fair Credit Reporting Act (FCRA)**

A U.S. federal law that promotes the accuracy, fairness, and privacy of consumer information contained in credit reports. The FCRA provides consumers with the right to access their credit information and dispute inaccuracies.

**Financial Literacy**

The ability to understand and effectively manage financial resources, including knowledge of financial products, consumer rights, and the implications of financial decisions. Financial literacy empowers consumers to make informed choices and protect their financial interests.

**Fractional Reserve Banking**

A banking system in which banks are required to keep only a fraction of their deposits as reserves, allowing them to lend out the remainder. This system enables banks to create credit and expand the money supply, but it also involves certain risks and regulatory oversight.

**Know-Your-Customer (KYC)**

A set of procedures used by banks and financial institutions to verify the identity of their customers. KYC regulations are designed to prevent fraud, money laundering, and other illicit activities by ensuring that banks have accurate information about their clients.

**Legal Aid**

Services provided to individuals who cannot afford to pay for legal representation. Legal aid organizations offer assistance in various legal matters, including banking disputes, to ensure access to justice for all consumers.

### Monetary Policy

The process by which a central bank manages the money supply and interest rates to achieve economic objectives, such as controlling inflation, maintaining employment, and ensuring financial stability. Monetary policy directly affects the availability and cost of credit.

### Ombudsman

An independent authority appointed to investigate and resolve complaints against financial institutions. Ombudsmen provide consumers with an impartial means of addressing grievances without resorting to litigation.

### Possession

In the context of banking, possession refers to the control or custody of financial assets, such as bank credits or securities. Legal possession is necessary for transferring ownership and ensuring the proper execution of financial transactions.

### Regulatory Framework

The system of laws, rules, and regulations that govern the operations of banks and financial institutions. The regulatory framework aims to ensure the stability, transparency, and integrity of the financial system while protecting consumers' rights.

### Smart Contracts

Self-executing contracts with the terms directly written into code, operating on blockchain technology. Smart contracts automatically enforce the terms of an agreement without the need for intermediaries, enhancing efficiency and reducing costs.

### Statute of Limitations

The legally defined time limit within which a claim or legal action must be filed. In banking disputes, the statute of limitations varies depending on the type of claim and jurisdiction, affecting the ability to pursue legal remedies.

### Unconscionability

A legal doctrine that allows courts to refuse to enforce contracts that are grossly unfair or oppressive. In banking, a contract may be deemed unconscionable if it imposes excessively harsh terms on the consumer, such as exorbitant fees or punitive interest rates.

### Unjust Enrichment

A legal principle that prevents one party from benefiting at the expense of another in an unfair or unjust manner. In banking, claims of unjust enrichment may arise when a customer receives funds or benefits they are not entitled to.

### Valuation

The process of determining the worth or value of financial assets, such as bank credits or securities. Accurate valuation is essential for assessing risk, making investment decisions, and ensuring fair transactions in the banking industry.

### Samples of Affidavits

Here are some samples of affidavits and legal documents that can be used in the context of banking and financial transactions. These documents serve as templates and should be customized according to specific legal requirements and the particular circumstances of each case.

### 1. Sample Affidavit of Payment Dispute

Affidavit of Payment Dispute

State of [State]

County of [County]

I, [Full Name], residing at [Full Address], being duly sworn, hereby depose and state the following under oath:

1. Affiant's Information

I am the account holder of a [type of account, e.g., checking/savings/ loan/credit card] account, account number [XXXX-XXXX-XXXX-XXXX], with [Bank Name], located at [Bank's Address].

2. Disputed Transaction Details

On or about [Date of Transaction], a transaction in the amount of [Amount] was posted to my account. This transaction is reflected as [Transaction Description] on my bank statement dated [Date of Statement].

3. Nature of Dispute

I dispute this transaction on the grounds that [briefly describe the reason for the dispute; for example, "the transaction was unauthorized," "I did not receive the goods/services," "the transaction amount is incorrect," etc.].

4. Attempts to Resolve the Dispute

I have made several attempts to resolve this matter with [Bank Name] by [describe actions taken, such as "calling customer service," "sending emails," "visiting the branch," etc.] on [list dates]. Despite these efforts, the issue remains unresolved.

5. Supporting Documentation

Attached hereto are copies of the relevant bank statements, correspondence, and any other documentation that supports my claim. These documents are true and correct copies of the originals.

6. Statement of Truth

I hereby declare under penalty of perjury that the foregoing is true and correct to the best of my knowledge and belief.

Signature of Affiant: ______________________________

Date: ______________________________

Sworn to and subscribed before me,

this (xxxxx) day of (xxxxx),20(xxxxx).

Notary Public

My Commission Expires: (xxxxx)

## 2. Sample Affidavit of Unauthorized Transaction

Affidavit of Unauthorized Transaction

State of [State]

County of [County]

I, [Full Name], residing at [Full Address], being duly sworn, depose and state the following:

1. Personal Information

I am the primary account holder of a [type of account] account with [Bank Name], account number [XXXX-XXXX-XXXX-XXXX].

2. Details of the Unauthorized Transaction

On [Date of Transaction], an unauthorized transaction in the amount of [Amount] was made using my account. This transaction was processed as [Transaction Type, e.g., debit card purchase, ATM withdrawal, etc.] at [Merchant/Location].

3. Absence of Authorization

At no time did I authorize or consent to this transaction. Furthermore, my debit/credit card and account information were in my possession at the time the unauthorized transaction was made.

4. Immediate Actions Taken

Upon discovering the unauthorized transaction, I immediately notified [Bank Name] on [Date], and reported the matter to their fraud department. My account was subsequently frozen to prevent further unauthorized use.

5. Report to Law Enforcement

A report of this unauthorized transaction has been filed with the [Name of Law Enforcement Agency], case number [Case Number], on [Date of Report]. A copy of the report is attached.

6. Statement of Non-Involvement

I affirm that I did not participate in or benefit from this transaction in any way, and I have no knowledge of the person(s) responsible for it.

7. Affirmation

I affirm that the statements in this affidavit are true and correct to the best of my knowledge and belief.

Signature of Affiant: (xxxxx)

Date: (xxxxx)

Sworn to and subscribed before me,

this (xxxxx) day of (xxxxx) 20(xxxxx)

Notary Public

My Commission Expires: (xxxxx)

### 3. Sample Promissory Note

Promissory Note

Date: [Date]

Principal Amount: $[Amount]

Interest Rate: [Interest Rate]% per annum

For value received, the undersigned, [Borrower's Full Name], of [Borrower's Address], (hereinafter referred to as "Borrower"), hereby promises to pay to the order of [Lender's Full Name], of [Lender's Address], (hereinafter referred to as "Lender"), the principal sum of [Amount in Words] Dollars ($[Amount in Numbers]), together with interest on the unpaid principal balance at the rate of [Interest Rate]% per annum.

1. Payment Terms

The Borrower shall make payments of principal and interest in [number of payments] installments of $[Amount of Each Payment] each, beginning on [Start Date] and continuing on the [day] day of each month thereafter until the principal and interest are fully paid.

2. Prepayment

The Borrower may prepay this Note, in whole or in part, without penalty, at any time.

3. Default

If the Borrower fails to make any payment due under this Note, the entire unpaid principal balance and any accrued interest shall become immediately due and payable at the option of the Lender.

4. Governing Law

This Note shall be governed by and construed in accordance with the laws of the State of [State].

5. Severability

If any provision of this Note is found to be unenforceable, all other provisions will remain in full force and effect.

Borrower's Signature: (xxxxx)

Printed Name: [Borrower's Full Name]

Date: (xxxxx)

Lender's Signature: (xxxxx)

Printed Name: [Lender's Full Name]

Date: (xxxxx)

### 4. Sample Power of Attorney for Banking Transactions

Power of Attorney for Banking Transactions

I, [Principal's Full Name], residing at [Principal's Address], hereby appoint [Agent's Full Name], residing at [Agent's Address], as my true and lawful attorney-in-fact, to act in my name and on my behalf in matters relating to my bank accounts with [Bank Name], account number(s) [List Account Numbers].

Powers Granted:

1. Deposit and Withdraw Funds: To deposit and withdraw funds from my bank accounts.

2. Sign Checks and Drafts: To sign checks, drafts, and other instruments in my name.

3. Access Safe Deposit Boxes: To access and manage the contents of my safe deposit box, if applicable.

4. Obtain Financial Information: To obtain statements, passbooks, and other financial information.

5. Conduct Transactions: To conduct any banking transactions, including electronic transfers, as I could personally perform.

Effective Date and Duration:

This Power of Attorney shall take effect immediately and shall remain in effect until [Specify Date] or until revoked by me in writing.

Revocation:

I reserve the right to revoke this Power of Attorney at any time. Any such revocation shall be effective upon receipt by [Agent's Full Name].

Signature of Principal: (xxxxx)

Printed Name: [Principal's Full Name]

Date: (xxxxx)

Acknowledgment

State of [State]

County of [County]

On this (xxxxx) day of (xxxxx) 20(xxxxx) before me, the undersigned Notary Public, personally appeared [Principal's Full Name], who proved to me on the basis of satisfactory evidence to be the person whose name is subscribed to the within instrument, and acknowledged that he/she executed the same.

Notary Public

My Commission Expires: (xxxxx)

### 5. Sample Demand Letter for Breach of Contract

[Your Name]

[Your Address]

[City, State, Zip Code]

[Email Address]

[Phone Number]

[Date]

[Recipient's Name]

[Recipient's Title/Position]

[Bank Name]

[Bank's Address]

[City, State, Zip Code]

Re: Breach of Contract – [Contract Name/Number]

Dear [Recipient's Name],

I am writing to formally notify [Bank Name] of a breach of contract regarding [describe the nature of the contract, e.g., loan agreement, mortgage, etc.], dated [Date of Contract], between myself and [Bank Name].

Specifically, [describe the breach in detail, e.g., "On [Date], I discovered that the interest rate on my loan was increased without notice or my consent, contrary to the terms outlined in Section [X] of the agreement."]

I have attached relevant documents that substantiate my claim, including a copy of the original contract and recent statements.

Remedy Sought

To resolve this matter, I request that [Bank Name] take the following actions:

1. [Specify the actions you want the bank to take, e.g., "Revert the interest rate to the agreed-upon percentage of [X]%."]

2. [Specify any additional remedies sought, e.g., "Provide a written confirmation that no further unauthorized changes will be made."]

I expect a written response to this letter within [specify a reasonable timeframe, e.g., "14 days"] from the date of receipt. If the matter is not resolved within this period, I may be compelled to pursue further legal action to enforce my rights under the contract, including seeking damages for any losses incurred due to the breach.

Please consider this letter a formal demand for the resolution of the aforementioned breach of contract. I hope to resolve this matter amicably and without further escalation.

Thank you for your prompt attention to this serious issue. I look forward to your immediate response.

Sincerely,

[Your Signature]

[Your Printed Name]

These sample affidavits and legal documents provide a foundation for various situations related to banking and financial transactions. It is important to consult with a legal professional when preparing and using these documents to ensure they meet all legal requirements and are appropriately customized for your specific circumstances.

### Checklist for Reviewing Bank Contracts

Reviewing a bank contract carefully before signing is crucial to understanding your rights and obligations, avoiding potential pitfalls, and ensuring the terms align with your financial interests. Use this checklist to guide you through the process of reviewing bank contracts, such as loan agreements, credit card terms, deposit accounts, and other financial services.

1. Verify Your Personal Information

- Ensure your name, address, and other personal details are accurate.

- Check that the account number or any other unique identifiers are correct.

2. Understand the Contract Type and Purpose

- Identify the type of contract (e.g., loan agreement, credit card terms, deposit account).

- Confirm the purpose of the contract and that it matches your understanding.

3. Review Interest Rates and Fees

- Interest Rate: Check the interest rate (fixed or variable) and understand how it is calculated.

- APR (Annual Percentage Rate): Review the APR, which includes the interest rate and any additional fees.

- Fees: Look for any associated fees, such as application fees, annual fees, late payment fees, overdraft fees, or prepayment penalties.

4. Understand the Repayment Terms

- Payment Schedule: Review the payment schedule, including the frequency (monthly, quarterly, etc.) and due dates.

- Minimum Payment: Understand the minimum payment requirements and how payments are applied to the principal and interest.

- Late Payment Penalties: Check for any late payment penalties or increased interest rates after a missed payment.

5. Check for Collateral Requirements

- Determine if the contract requires any form of collateral (e.g., a car, home, or savings account) to secure the loan.

- Understand what happens to the collateral in the event of default.

6. Read the Default and Termination Clauses

- Default Conditions: Identify what constitutes a default (e.g., missed payments, insufficient funds, breach of terms).

- Termination Rights: Review both parties' rights to terminate the contract and the conditions under which termination can occur.

7. Examine the Dispute Resolution Process

- Arbitration Clause: Check if the contract includes an arbitration clause, requiring disputes to be resolved outside of court.

- Legal Jurisdiction: Understand which state or country's laws will govern the contract in the event of a dispute.

8. Look for Clauses About Changes in Terms

- Review any clauses that allow the bank to change the terms of the contract unilaterally.

- Understand how and when you will be notified of any changes.

9. Understand the Rights and Obligations of Both Parties

- Your Obligations: Clearly understand your responsibilities under the contract (e.g., making timely payments, maintaining insurance).

- Bank's Obligations: Review what services the bank is obligated to provide and any guarantees they offer.

10. Identify Consumer Protection Clauses

- Check for clauses that protect your rights, such as those related to data privacy, fraud protection, and error resolution.

- Understand your right to cancel the contract within a certain period, if applicable.

11. Review Terms for Special Promotions

- If there are promotional offers (e.g., zero-interest periods, cashback rewards), understand the conditions and expiration dates.

- Know what happens when the promotional period ends.

12. Examine Cross-Default Clauses

- Determine if defaulting on one loan or credit line automatically places you in default on others with the same bank.

13. Check for Prepayment and Early Payoff Terms

- Understand any prepayment penalties or restrictions on early loan payoff.

- Review any benefits or rebates for paying off the loan early.

14. Scrutinize Any Guarantees or Co-Signer Responsibilities

- If a guarantor or co-signer is involved, understand their obligations and liabilities.

- Ensure that all parties named in the contract agree to the terms.

15. Check for Any Conditions Precedent

- Review any conditions that must be met before the contract becomes effective (e.g., proof of income, insurance coverage).

16. Confirm Clarity and Language

- Ensure the language is clear, precise, and free of legal jargon.

- Ask for clarification of any terms or clauses you do not understand.

17. Review for Hidden Clauses or Fine Print

- Read through the entire contract, including any fine print, to avoid missing important details.

- Be cautious of clauses that seem one-sided or overly favorable to the bank.

18. Verify the Complete Agreement

- Confirm that all discussed terms are included in the written contract and that there are no additional verbal agreements.

- Ensure all appendices, schedules, and referenced documents are included and understood.

19. Seek Professional Advice

- If you have any doubts or need further clarification, consider consulting with a financial advisor or attorney before signing.

20. Ensure Both Parties Sign the Contract

- Verify that the contract is signed by both you and a representative of the bank.

- Keep a copy of the signed contract for your records.

By following this checklist, you can better protect yourself and ensure that you fully understand the terms and conditions of your banking contract.